Original title:
Tropical Sunrise

Copyright © 2025 Creative Arts Management OÜ
All rights reserved.

Author: Jude Lancaster
ISBN HARDBACK: 978-1-80581-528-0
ISBN PAPERBACK: 978-1-80581-055-1
ISBN EBOOK: 978-1-80581-528-0

Onto the Shore, the Light Bows

Morning creeps with giggles and sighs,
A sleepy sun in the jellyfish skies.
Crabs wear their shells like party hats,
While seagulls drop fries like fluffy spats.

Waves clap their hands and dance, oh so spry,
But my coffee's more wild than the gulls up high.
Sandcastles splash down with a comical crash,
As I slip on a sea noodle, oh what a splash!

Reflections in the Misty Sea

The sea looks like a mirror, all foggy and fun,
Where fish wear their sunglasses and bask in the sun.
A dolphin flips pancakes, quite absurd in its flair,
While I trip on a starfish, it gives me a stare.

Seagulls submit to yoga, all zen on a rock,
While the waves crash like tickles, they endlessly mock.
The sun paints each ripple with colors so bright,
I snort as a crab gives me a funny fright!

Awakening the Earth with Color

The plants wake up sleepy, but what's that they smell?
Is it coffee? No, it's just jellybean gel.
Flowers wear socks in a colorful spree,
While worms host a disco, just for me.

The skies throw confetti, like it's someone's birthday,
But I'm stuck in my hammock, enjoying the sway.
The earth spins in giggles, as colors collide,
While I chuckle at bees in their fuzzy pride.

The Unfurling of Radiant Petals

Petals unfold like secrets, with laughter and cheer,
They dance on the breeze, all the plants squeeze near.
The flowers have jokes, they whisper and tease,
While the sun rolls his eyes, shining down with ease.

A bumblebee winks, like he's rounded a bend,
He bumps into daisies, his awkward best friend.
With a sprinkle of pollen, they break into rhyme,
I can't help but giggle, it's flower prime time!

The Dawn Whispers Secrets of the Sea

At dawn, the seagulls squawk and squeal,
Crabs dance a jig, on their tiny heels.
The ocean winks, a glittering tease,
Tickling the sand with a soft, cool breeze.

Fish flip flops in a breakfast show,
While dolphins laugh, putting on a row.
Shells gossip secrets, a clattering sound,
As the sun chuckles, warming the ground.

Illuminated Dreams of the Dawn

Light spills like syrup, a golden delight,
Birds wear their pajamas, still groggy from night.
The flowers yawn wide, stretching with glee,
While butterflies giggle and sip on their tea.

Clouds dress in fluff, a cozy array,
As a rooster croons, 'It's time to play!'
The light flickers on like a cheeky prank,
Even the trees seem to shake and prank.

The Daybreak Mosaic of Nature

Colors collide in a whimsical dance,
Squirrels in top hats, giving chance a glance.
The sun doodles rays on the canvas blue,
While lizards strut like they've got a clue.

The sky's a confetti, a playful spree,
Waves whisper jokes, splashing in glee.
Bees zipping around, humming a tune,
While frogs croak along, crooning to the moon.

A Choreography of Light and Breeze

Breezes waltz in a lively spin,
While the sun plays peekaboo, wearing a grin.
Palm trees sway as if they know a joke,
A performance sweet, no word left unspoke.

The shadows stretch long, they bend and twirl,
As fireflies giggle, making the world whirl.
Crickets chirp rhythm, a raucous beat,
In this morning dance, the day feels so sweet.

First Light on Palm Fronds

As daylight peeks from behind the trees,
The iguana yawns and stretches with ease.
Coconuts drop with a loud, funny thud,
Even the crabs seem to dance in the mud.

Bikinis are flipped like pancakes in sun,
While laughter erupts, oh, isn't it fun?
Bright colors splash as the seabirds take flight,
That's what happens when day turns to night.

Luminous Kisses on Silken Shores

The waves giggle softly, tickling the sand,
Footprints are scattered, a jolly band.
Tanned tourists chase crabs with shouts of delight,
While sunscreen splatters in a comical fight.

Shells play peek-a-boo in the foamy embrace,
Starfish join in for a sunbathing race.
Laughter erupts as someone gets splashed,
In this morning dance, no fun can be stashed.

The Breath of Morning Mist

Misty tendrils weave through the trees with a grin,
While roosters wake up, noon's just a spin.
Pineapple hats, a sight to behold,
As locals debate if the weather is cold.

Waves are at play, kicking sand in surprise,
Seagulls wear shades, oh, what a disguise!
Everyone smiles as the day comes alive,
In laughter and chaos, it's where we all thrive.

Echoes of Dawn in the Breeze

Dancing palm fronds sway to a beat in the air,
With parrots that gossip, oh, do they declare!
The sun's lazy stretch, a warm, giggly gleam,
Makes everyone wonder if this is a dream.

Beach balls bounce high, like joyful balloons,
Kids build sandcastles, while humming old tunes.
A flip-flop flips, and an umbrella takes flight,
Under this jolly, mischievous light.

Awakening the Island Fables

The roosters crow like they own the place,
Squawking secrets of the sun's embrace.
Lemurs swing from branches high,
Chasing dreams as they pass by.

Bananas slip beneath bare feet,
While monkeys rehearse a morning beat.
Palm trees sway, their shadows dance,
As surfboards wait for a wild romance.

Nature's Brushstrokes at Daybreak

A painter's clasping the sky so wide,
With colors splashing like a joyful ride.
An iguana dons shades to bask,
While flip-flops launch a daring task.

Sea turtles race, oh what a sight,
Chasing seabirds in midday flight.
Coconuts roll like a beach ball game,
Each wave welcomes the laugh of fame.

Serene Skies, Whispering Dawn

The clouds gossip, a fluffy parade,
Whispering tales that never fade.
A crab tiptoes with a silly strut,
While surfers dream of the perfect cut.

Fish flip-flop in giggly delight,
As fishermen grumble, 'out of sight!'
The sun peeks in, with a quirky grin,
Startled flamingos begin to spin.

A Symphony of Colors Unfolds

A band of birds starts the day with a song,
While palm leaves twirl to a rhythm so strong.
Bamboos nod as if in glee,
And crabs clap their claws for all to see.

The waves chuckle, a jolly sight,
As beaches summon a picnic delight.
A parrot pipes jokes from atop a tree,
Cheers to the day we all agree!

First Flare Over Distant Horizons

A bright orange ball, pops up with a grin,
The world yawns and stretches, where do we begin?
Birds in their feathers, do a silly parade,
One plays a trumpet, the other's delayed!

Coffee cups tremble, as mugs align,
While squirrels debate if it's their time to shine.
The sun's got an ego, it's shining so bright,
And everyone's laughing at morning's first light.

Blooms Unfolding to Warmth

Flowers wake slowly, with petals of glee,
They giggle at ants, like 'What's wrong with thee?'
Buds stretch and blossom, they take off their sheets,
Saying, 'Look at us now, we're the freshest of treats!'

The bees buzz in circles, they dance all around,
While hiccuping frogs make the silliest sound.
Colors collide like a playful surprise,
Botanical jokes fill the clear morning skies.

Celestial Dance Above Emerald Isles

Stars got tired, they took a quick nap,
While cloud pillows fluffed, all snug in a cap.
A parrot yelled 'squawk', as the moon did a twirl,
The heavens were laughing, they gave it a whirl!

Comets are sliding, like socks on the floor,
While planets are arguing, 'Who's first to explore?'
Milky Way giggles with a sprinkle of light,
As everyone winks in the warmth of the night.

Waves of Light Breaking the Night

Laughter spills over like waves on the shore,
The night's tired jokes, we've all heard before.
Shells gather round, with their tales to relay,
And crabs take to dancing, in their jolly ballet.

Lights in the surf, do a shimmy and shake,
While shadows conspire, and the beach seems to wake.
The sun takes a bow, with a chuckle so bright,
Waving goodbye to the lingering night!

Serenity Beneath the Turning Sky

Beneath the sky that swirls like cream,
The palm trees dance, a comic dream.
A coconut drops with a thud so loud,
While parrots gossip, forming a crowd.

Waves wave back like they're in a play,
Each splash a joke that drips from the bay.
The sun yawns wide, stretching its rays,
While sandcastles giggle in sandy displays.

Laughter floats on the warm, sweet breeze,
A joyful chorus from buzzing bees.
Flip-flops squeak as they join the fray,
While a crab moonwalks, come what may.

So sip that drink, with a silly straw,
As the sun dips low, casting its jaw.
With each silly moment and funky style,
Let's toast to dawn with a goofy smile!

Echoes of Radiance in Quiet Boughs

In branches thick, where shadows play,
A sloth hangs upside down, what a display.
A parrot squawks with a mighty flair,
And all the monkeys giggle, without a care.

Light bursts forth in a cheerful race,
A turtle strolls at a comical pace.
Mangoes tumble, rolling around,
While flowers wink and look profound.

With each ray a wink, each cloud a jest,
The jungle's humor is always the best.
A squirrel juggles nuts in a spree,
While the frogs croak out a rhapsody.

So relish the laughter that mornings bring,
To the rhythm of life, let's happily sing.
In nature's circus, find joy and bliss,
As each waking moment is one you won't miss!

A World Waking to Color

The canvas stretches, painted bright,
Emerald leaves spark under light.
A toucan's beak, a rainbow's arc,
Plays peek-a-boo with the dawn's sweet spark.

Bumblebees buzz with a jiggy beat,
As flowers twerk to the morning heat.
A lizard lounges, sporting shades,
While in the sun, a chameleon's plays.

Each color splashes with giggly cheer,
As butterflies flutter, drawing near.
The sky's a canvas of beckoning hues,
Spilling its laughter in dazzling views.

So let's prance in this parade divine,
For every dawn holds a punchline fine.
In this world where silly reigns supreme,
Awake to color, live the dream!

Morning Light's Tender Embrace

As morning light sneaks through the blinds,
A sleepy cat stretches, oh, what finds!
An ant parade marches in line,
While a turtle takes his sweet, slow time.

The goldfish bubble, plotting a scheme,
While sunbeams giggle in a gleaming beam.
Dewdrops twinkle on the grass like jewels,
As crickets tune their morning school.

With each chirp a punchline, crisp and neat,
The rooster crows with a certain beat.
Bacon sizzling plays breakfast's tune,
As laughter dances to the rising moon.

So let's embrace this day's sweet charm,
With giggles and grins, no cause for alarm.
Wrapped up in light, with a wink and a sigh,
In a world of fun, let's soar and fly!

Joyful Whispers in the Air

Bright colors splash and play,
The roosters dance at break of day.
With coffee cups and dreams to chase,
We giggle on our waking face.

A parrot sings a silly tune,
While monkeys slide from noon to moon.
Ocean waves in playful rush,
Tickle toes with a frothy hush.

Sunlit Pathways of the Heart

Beneath the palm, we take our stand,
With sandy toes and drink in hand.
The sunbeams tease, like playful sprites,
As flip-flops fly in joyful flights.

A crab in haste, it scuttles fast,
While we throw laughter, none surpassed.
The world's a stage with wacky scenes,
Where fun unfolds in brilliant greens.

Lush Vistas in Gentle Gaze

The flowers wear a rainbow crown,
As bees zoom by, they spin and frown.
The breeze brings whispers of delight,
While lizards bask in morning light.

Banana peels in stealthy way,
Make wanderers slip, then laugh and stay.
With giggles shared, we roam and play,
In this wild dance, we lose our way.

The Mirth of a New Day

The sun may rise with laughter loud,
While nature bounces, feeling proud.
Each leaf a tickle, each breeze a jest,
In this bright world, we're truly blessed.

A turtle winks with wisdom rare,
As cheeky monkeys leap in air.
We stretch our arms in sunny waves,
Embracing joy that adventure paves.

Glimmers of Gold on the Water

The sun jumped out, did a silly dance,
Casting sparkles like glitter in a trance.
Fish put on hats, they swam in a line,
Giggling bubbles, they felt so divine.

Palm trees swayed, joining in the fun,
With coconuts laughing at each little pun.
The ocean wore shades, such a dapper sight,
Waves all applauded the morning light.

Echoes of Light in the Jungle

Monkeys wore shades, swinging high with glee,
Chasing after beams, as bright as can be.
Parrots yelled jokes, colorful and loud,
They formed a comedy club, so proud.

The sun peeked in, with a twinkle and wink,
Slipping through leaves, making jungle animals think.
Snakes in bow ties, oh what a scene,
All critters laughing, feeling so keen.

Shoreside Serenade at Day's Break

Sandcastles chuckled as the tide rolled in,
Their towers all giggled with each little grin.
Seagulls worked hard, doing stand-up routines,
While crabs told jokes in their sandy machines.

Waves clapped their hands, a cheer so loud,
Shells joined the chorus, forming a crowd.
The breeze spun tales of food and delight,
As everyone sang to the morning light.

Celestial Brushstrokes on the Horizon

The dawn dipped its brush in a jar of bright cheer,
Painting the clouds with colors so clear.
Stars take a bow, as they fade from the show,
Leaving the skies all aglow with a glow.

The moon laughed lightly, for it had to go,
Leaving behind tales of night's silly flow.
As the sun cracked up, the world came awake,
Every creature joined in for day's big break.

Dawn's Embrace in Paradise

The sun peeks in, a golden tease,
Lizards dance with quick little knees.
Coconuts roll like tricks from a hat,
Palm trees sway, just look at that!

Chickens sing in a clucky tune,
While roosters boast, they think they're the moon.
Sand crabs scuttle in a hasty race,
Oh, morning mess, what a funny place!

A parrot squawks a gossip spree,
About a neighbor's lost cup of tea.
As waves giggle on the shore,
Seems like fun is never a bore!

Dawn wraps jokes in its soft light,
Even the fishes are feeling bright.
So come join us, let laughter rise,
In this silly dance beneath the skies!

Whispering Palms at First Light

A soft whisper from the trees,
As if they're giggling in a breeze.
Sunshine spills in a joyful splash,
While sleepy crabs perform a dash.

Seagulls argue about breakfast fare,
Landing with grace like they just don't care.
A beach ball rolls, oh what a trip,
Chasing it down, that's a funny script!

The waves are ticklish, can you feel?
They tickle toes like a playful seal.
And the sunrise shows its silly face,
Painting the sky with a grand embrace!

So let's wear shades while we laugh and play,
This cheeky morn will brighten our day.
With laughter ringing and smiles all around,
In the light of the day, joy is found!

A Canvas of Coral Skies

A splash of colors, a painter's dream,
The sun yawns wide with a playful beam.
Marshmallow clouds float by so free,
As if they've come for a little spree.

Fishy friends swim in a bubble parade,
While crabs usher in with their crabby charade.
Every splash is a giggle, a joke to share,
On this coral canvas hung in midair!

As surfers stumble with grand applause,
They're part of the art, oh what a cause!
With each wave crashing like a slinky toy,
Laughter bubbles up, oh what a joy!

So wave at the sun, and wink at the tide,
In this masterpiece where laughter won't hide.
Every sunrise brings color anew,
In this silly show where fun is the glue!

Awakening the Ocean's Heart

The ocean yawns, its heart in bliss,
With giggles and bubbles, who could resist?
A seal pops up with a clumsy cheer,
Whispering waves bring laughter near.

The jellyfish jive like they're in a trance,
While dolphins leap for the morning dance.
Waves tickle toes where the sand runs wild,
Nature's own game, oh how we smiled!

Seashells gossip on the golden shore,
Trading tall tales of the ocean's lore.
A crab with shades strikes a silly pose,
In this ocean party, everyone knows!

So rise with the sun, let the fun unwind,
With silly hearts, let your worries be blind.
In laughter and light, we'll forever stay,
As the ocean's heart awakens and plays!

Untamed Beauty in Golden Glow

The roosters crow like they're on stage,
Their feathered outfits, quite the rage!
Palm trees sway in a dance so bold,
While monkeys sing of stories untold.

Sunbeams peek through leaves with cheer,
Even the iguanas stop to leer!
Nature's gossip fills the air,
In this morning square, there's laughter to share.

Reflections in a Warm Breeze

The breeze tickles at noses and toes,
As flip-flops flop, and the ocean glows.
Seagulls squawk with a comedic flair,
While beach balls bounce without a care.

A crab with attitude scuttles ahead,
Waving pincers like he's been fed!
Sandcastles rise, then fall with a splash,
As kids dive in for a sunny bash.

The Fanfare of a New Dawn

Confetti clouds parade in the sky,
While dolphins leap, oh my, oh my!
A sun with a grin peeks over the bay,
"Let's party!" it shouts in a golden ray.

Coconuts cheer, all dressed for the ball,
As the ocean's tune makes everyone sprawl.
Leaves rustle like giggles in the heat,
As laughter rolls in with the rhythmic beat.

Aromas of Coffee and Sun

The rich brew brews like a potion of cheer,
As sleepy heads rise up from yesteryear.
With mugs in hand, smiles spread wide,
Like a parade where no one can hide.

Sipping joy with toes in the sand,
A pirate's breakfast, oh isn't it grand?
With each hearty laugh, the day jumps alive,
In this warm brew, all souls thrive.

Sunlit Canopies and Serene Waves

Amidst the palms, the squirrels prance,
Coffee cups spill in a morning dance.
Seagulls tease with raucous calls,
While flip-flops fly, as laughter falls.

Coconuts roll, a game they play,
Shadows stretching under the bay.
A hammock swings with giggles bright,
As the sun chases away the night.

Bright umbrellas pop like flowers bloom,
And beach balls bounce like kids in a room.
We chase our hats, they take a flight,
In this sunny circus, what pure delight!

Lizards blink with a stylish flair,
While we attempt the perfect hair.
A world where fun's just a wave away,
In golden beams, we laugh and sway.

Citrus Dreams in the Golden Hour

Oranges giggle in morning dew,
Bananas slip on their bright yellow shoe.
Lemons join in, tart jokes they weave,
As mangoes wink, you'd hardly believe.

Juices flow in a zesty spree,
While we dance 'round like fruit on a spree.
A pineapple wearing shades so cool,
Says, "Surfs up, let's break every rule!"

Papayas laugh, their colors so bold,
In this fruity fiesta, stories unfold.
A slice of toast, a jig, and a spin,
As daybreak smiles, let the antics begin!

With each bright beam, sweetness ignites,
Mimicking sunbeams, oh what delights!
Lemonade games and jelly-filled dreams,
In this cheery world, nothing's as it seems!

Harmony of Light and Shadow

Geckos play tag on sun-kissed stone,
While shadows stretch in a lazy tone.
The parrot squawks with a cheeky flair,
As a beach ball bounces through the air.

Flip-flops slapping a rhythm profound,
Echoing laughter that echoes around.
Even the sun wears a goofy grin,
Painting the world in a dance of skin.

Mirrored reflections on playful tides,
With sandcastles leaning, oh what pride!
And crabs doing the cha-cha with glee,
As surfboards wink from the edge of the sea.

In this realm where sun and mischief blend,
Fun comes easy, it's all just pretend.
So, grab your partner and let's take flight,
In this merry mix of day and night!

A Symphony of Color at Daybreak

Colors collide as dawn breaks free,
Like a painter's chase through a tropical spree.
Flamingos flaunt their ruffled feather show,
As we giggle at nature's wild tableau.

The ocean winks in shades of light,
While jellyfish float in a dream-like flight.
Crisp air whispers jokes to the sun,
As rainbow fruit salads have just begun.

Tropical flowers join the parade,
Their scents colliding in vibrant cascade.
We play tag with the splashes and rolls,
Chasing the laughter that bubbles and strolls.

With each new hue, the silliness grows,
Even the seaweed joins in the shows.
So let's toast to this bright, goofy dawn,
Where joy dances freely until it's all gone!

Embers of Morning Over Flora and Fauna.

As dawn breaks with a wink and a giggle,
The parrot squawks, 'I'm ready to wiggle!'
A lizard in shades does a morning dance,
As bees hum along, giving flowers a chance.

The sun peeks shyly, its rays all a-flutter,
While monkeys swing low, laughing with their butter.
A cricket tries crooning, but hits a wrong note,
As the whole jungle wakes up, in a funny little boat.

Palm trees are swaying, a comical sight,
They're cracking their backs, ready for flight.
The iguana grins, 'Oh, what a fine day!'
While the sloth just yawns, 'I'm not on my way.'

So here's to the morn, with its silly routine,
Where every creature is part of the scene.
With laughter and joy, let the frolic begin,
In this thriving realm, where wide smiles spin.

Radiance over Ocean Waves

The sun shows up, with its big golden grin,
Dancing on waves, letting laughter begin.
A crab wearing shades struts down the shore,
While the fish under bubbles giggle and roar.

The waves clap their hands with splashes of cheer,
While snorkelers sing like they don't have a fear.
A dolphin does flips, making quite the splash,
While seagulls dive-bomb, hoping for a snack dash.

Sun hats are flying, umbrellas turn wild,
Sandcastle builders, each like a child.
The wind takes a tug, starting a sneeze,
Making everyone laugh, as they brush off the breeze.

So here on the coast, where the fun never ends,
Each sparkle of light brings laughter, my friends.
With each wave that crashes, let giggles arise,
For the ocean's great charm is found in surprise.

Dawn's Embrace in Paradise

The sun rolls in, with a playful nudge,
Tickling the trees, refusing to budge.
A toucan chuckles, with colors so bright,
While the slithering snake checks its scales for a bite.

With each cheeky ray, the flowers do bloom,
Turning their heads and shaking off gloom.
A swing from a vine sparks laughter and cheer,
As frogs pick up rhythm, croaking loud in the near.

Bright butterflies join the hoot and the holler,
They flap in a circle, like a floral baller.
The breeze carries giggles from the hills to the bay,
Where laughter is tossed like confetti at play.

In this embrace, where day meets night's jest,
Every critter joins in, feeling quite blessed.
With joy in the air and warmth in our souls,
Mirth is the anthem, as the day swells and rolls.

Golden Hues of Morning Light

The sun stretches wide, giving the world a wink,
While the roosters all chuckle, "Come, it's time to think!"
A squirrel in pajamas leaps up to say,
'It's a funny old morning, come out and play!'

In fields of sweet laughter, the daisies spin,
As butterflies wink with their cheeky little grin.
A goat on a hill, with a hat slightly askew,
Sings, 'I'm fashionable, don't you think so too?'

The sunbeams tickle, bringing joy to each face,
As everyone giggles in this sunlit place.
With shadows that dance, and the leaves that cheer,
It's the perfect backdrop for a whimsical affair.

So let's skip along, with our hearts feeling bright,
In the golden glow of this marvelous light.
Where laughter's our compass, and joy finds a way,
To make each moment the best of our day.

The Dawn's Pulsing Heartbeat

Roosters crow with zest and cheer,
As bright rays tickle sleepy deer.
The coffee pot begins to dance,
In jammies, we prance, oh what a chance!

Waves giggle, splashing on the shore,
As seagulls squawk, demanding more.
The sun yawns wide, a golden grin,
A funny start, let the day begin!

Palm trees sway, their leaves aflutter,
While crabs do cha-cha through the butter.
Sandcastles rise with silly hats,
And dolphins giggle, wearing bats!

The morning air is fresh with spice,
Each moment's flavor, oh so nice.
With laughter echoing, joy ignites,
What silliness greets these sunny sights!

Whimsical Shadows on Soft Sands

Footprints trace a dancing jig,
Sandy shadows do a gig.
A coconut rolls by with glee,
It bumps my knee, oh what a spree!

Lizards sunbathe, oh my stars,
In shades of green, they twirl like cars.
Flip-flops flip, a silly tune,
Boogie-woogie, under the moon!

Seashells gossip, sharing a tale,
While breezes play a comic gale.
A hermit crab wears my lost shoe,
What's next? A crab dance? Who knew?

Laughter echoes from beach to beach,
Nature's comedy is within reach.
In shadows that twist and twine,
We find the funny in sunshine!

Glimmering Hopes in Soft Waves

The ocean sparkles like a joke,
A surfboard sails, but wait—kerploke!
A fish flops up, lands with a splash,
Winks at me, oh what a clash!

Dolphins play tag, chasing their tales,
While seaweed dances, swaying gales.
A crab in shades, oh what a sight,
Scuttling home before the night!

Waves whisper secrets, oh so sly,
Of mermaids giggling as they fly.
Jellyfish bob like balloons afloat,
As I try hard not to gloat!

Hope sparkles like glitter in foam,
In seaside laughter, we find our home.
Each wave a chuckle, each splash a cheer,
As the day dawns bright and clear!

Crescendo of Nature's Awakening

The symphony starts with a rooster's cry,
The sun peeks out with a sleepy sigh.
With each chirp, a melody builds,
As nature awakens, our laughter fills.

Coconut palms sway to the beat,
While ants march proud on tiny feet.
The ocean hums a jolly refrain,
As surf and sand share their disdain!

A kite flies high, twirling in air,
With children chasing without a care.
A piñata hangs from a palm so tall,
But bats and dreams will cause a fall!

Nature's concert plays on repeat,
With every giggle a dancing feat.
In the morning light, we find our place,
With smiles and fun, we join the race!

Island Rhythms in Golden Hues

A parrot sings off-key, oh what a sight,
The monkeys dance, keeping spirits bright.
Palm trees sway to a wacky tune,
As roosters crow to the rhythm of the moon.

Bright coconuts roll down the sandy lane,
The crabs join in, a quirky parade train.
Sunshine spills like juice from a cup,
We laugh and giggle as we all get up.

Colorful fish swim in a synchrony dance,
They shimmy and shake, giving us a chance.
To join the party without any fuss,
In this island groove, who needs a bus?

With every dawn, a new joke to unfurl,
Like seashells scattered, laughter we hurl.
In this vibrant chaos, we find our bliss,
Golden hues embrace, who could resist?

Whispers of Serenity at First Light

The morning whispers secrets of the sea,
As sea turtles tease, saying "Come join me!"
Birds chirp gossip in the trees above,
While the sun peeks out, spreading a warm shove.

A flip-flop's lost, oh where could it be?
Did a crab run off with it, we agree.
Coffee spills, but who cares with flair,
As we dive into breakfast without a care.

The hammock sways, a perfect delight,
But watch out! Here comes a butterfly flight.
It lands on my nose, tickling me so,
Laughter erupts, watch my silly show!

In the soft sun's rays, we make our own fun,
Chasing shadows, oh we won't be outdone.
As the day starts anew, we share a smile,
With whispers of peace that stretch a mile.

A New Day's Invitation

The ocean calls, a bubbly invite,
"Come paddle with me, forget the fright!"
A jellyfish joins, with a wobbly spin,
We laugh at its moves, who needs to win?

In colors so bright, the surfboards await,
We hop on the waves; it's never too late.
A seagull squawks a peculiar cheer,
As we tumble and splash, with giggles to hear.

Breakfast surprise? A fruit-filled delight,
Pineapple hats? Who wore them last night?
We wear our best smiles as we munch away,
Life's just too funny at the break of day.

As laughter erupts like the popping tide,
We dance with the waves, nowhere to hide.
The day stretches out, adventures take flight,
An invitation to joy, what a glorious sight!

Embrace of Pink and Gold

The sun yawns wide, stretching its glow,
While fish in the sea put on a show.
They flip and they flounder, just for a laugh,
In this pastel light, they dance like a calf.

A crab wearing shades, oh what a scene,
With a towel in claws, living out a dream.
He sunbathes lazy, with style and grace,
Why chase after work? There's no need for a race!

We gather the fruits, in a grand buffet,
Bananas with sunglasses, "Come join the fray!"
As laughter spills out on this sandy stage,
Humor is timeless, not bound by age.

In the embrace of pink, and gold so bright,
We find the magic at the start of light.
Each moment a giggle, each breath a delight,
We toast to the day, it feels just right!

Awakening the Coral Dreams

A parrot squawks a tuneful cheer,
As crabs tiptoe, drawing near.
The starfish yawns, shakes off the sand,
While dolphins toss a beach ball grand.

Flip-flops flapping, what a sight,
Coconuts rolling left and right.
Seagulls gossip in the breeze,
About the antics of the bees.

Sunbeams stretch like lazy cats,
While beach umbrellas dodge the rats.
The little fish paint their scales,
With hidden jokes and silly tales.

So here we are, what a delight,
Waking up to morning light.
With giggles dancing on the sea,
The coral dreams are wild and free.

Beachfront Radiance

The sun spills orange on the sand,
While sandcastles stand like a band.
Palm trees sway, they wave hello,
As surfers line up, ready to go.

A coconut blinks, what a sight,
As octopuses have a swim fight.
With laughter ringing all around,
The funniest moments can be found.

Flip-flops squirt with every stomp,
As sunflowers dance, do the chomp.
The tide calls out, "Come take a ride!"
In waves where all our worries hide.

Sunblock slathers, a gooey mess,
But who can care? We'll still impress.
Let's prance away, let's laugh a song,
In beachfront radiance, we belong.

New Day's Caress on the Sea

A jellyfish jigs, quite the show,
While sea turtles cry, "Take it slow!"
The roosters crow with quirky flair,
As fish share secrets in ocean air.

Beach balls zoom with joyous zest,
While sand goes flying, kids on quest.
Sun hats high and laughter loud,
With sweetness rising like a cloud.

The tide ticks on, like a clock,
While flip-flops meld, they go for a walk.
With giggles echoing through the sand,
A new day's caress, it's simply grand.

Let's dance with shadows, let's jump and squeal,
Under the sun, we spin and reel.
In this playful world, we all agree,
Life is best by the deep blue sea.

Horizon's Palette: A Dreamer's Delight

Colors explode as the sun climbs high,
A flamingo poses, oh my, oh my!
Coconuts wave from trees so tall,
While beach critters have a beach ball brawl.

Waves tickle toes, laughter in the air,
As sunburns form without a care.
The sand feels warm, like a cozy hug,
While seagulls squawk, a curious bug.

Pinching crabs practice their dance,
As we sip smoothies, join the romance.
With sunsets painting dreams anew,
In this delight, we find our crew.

The day may fade, but oh, the fun!
With jelly-legged dances, we've just begun.
In horizon's palette, let laughter reign,
As we cherish the memories that never wane.

Serenity Wrapped in Morning Fog

The roosters crow as if they're stars,
Claiming victory over night's bizarre.
A flip-flop slaps on the narrow path,
Leaving behind sleepy giraffes' laugh.

The coffee pot's gone rogue again,
The cat's now eyeing the fridge with zen.
Toasters pop like fireworks in May,
As squirrels debate the best way to play.

Fog dances slow, like a beachside jig,
While seagulls gossip, it's rather big.
The sun peeks out, a golden prank,
Now everyone's late for the cinnamon tank.

I trip over flip-flops while chasing dreams,
In a world where nothing's quite as it seems.
Such chaos brings smiles, joy on the go,
In the morning fog, we all take it slow.

Rhythms of the Rising Light

The sun winks cheekily from behind a cloud,
As night-time's secrets gather all proud.
Bacon sizzles like a record in spin,
While the dog performs a melodious grin.

The surfboards wait, lined up in a row,
Like kids at school, waiting to go.
Dance moves in sand, now shifting and spry,
With every wave crashing, we start to fly.

Umbrellas flip in a spunky ballet,
A sunburn's the price we just love to pay.
For parasails soaring look just like kites,
Tangled hair's close to new heights, a sight!

As jellyfish twirl in the playful tide,
We shake our heads, let laughter collide.
The morning's bliss wrapped in sunshine's glow,
Let's surf through life's rhythms, just go with the flow.

An Aria of Waves and Wind

There's a symphony only nature can play,
As waves perform tricks, come out and sway.
The beach ball bounces with a comedic thud,
And crabs hold auditions for a dance in the mud.

Whispers of wind tickle my toes,
While clams throw parties in glittering rows.
Birds sing pop tunes from high in the sky,
And I think to join but my dance moves just shy.

Kites dive and swoop, with flair on the run,
Fueling giggles while we bask in the fun.
Sea urchins chuckle as they roll on the shore,
With a prickle and laugh, they offer no more.

The ocean's drama unfolds its grand weave,
Where joy's a card game, you've just got to believe.
Each wave brings a story, each breeze a song,
Here we laugh together, right where we belong.

Celestial Glow Upon the Bay

Morning breaks with a splash of delight,
Asanemones wave hello in the light.
A fisherman's snore fills the marshmallow air,
While sandcastles rise without worry or care.

The dolphins plot tricks for the unsuspecting,
While shadows of turtles seek deep collecting.
Laughter erupts like fizz in a drink,
As beachgoers mingle and pause to think.

The sun cracks jokes, all jokes made of light,
While flip-flops unite, uniting the fight.
Each saucy wave brings a chuckle anew,
And a crab in a bowtie pops by for a view.

With a toss of the hair and a wink that is tight,
We admire the antics at the edge of the sight.
With each rising moment, new laughs take their flight,
In the warm glow of dawn, life feels just right.

Bounty of Color Befits the Day

The roosters crow with flair, they sing,
Their early tune is quite the thing.
The sun peeks out, a golden grin,
A bright-eyed cheer, let day begin!

Bamboo sways, the breeze does tease,
It tickles noses, oh what a breeze!
A parrot shouts, "Where's my breakfast?"
While monkeys swing, feeling quite blessed!

Fluffy clouds parade, no time for worry,
They race each other, oh what a flurry!
The palm trees sway, in silly dance,
Inviting all to join the prance!

So let's rejoice, with drinks in hand,
And toast to the joy of this bright land.
A funny start, with laughter's call,
In this color-filled morn, we have it all!

The Waking World and its Secrets

The night slips away, like a breaded snail,
The sun rolls out, oh what a tale!
Monkeys chuckle, as if they know,
All the secrets the daylight will show.

Coconut drops with a rumbling thud,
While crabs dance sideways, shuffling in mud.
Insects buzz in an orchestra's tease,
A hum of life, they giggle with ease!

Frogs croak jokes, in a swampy delight,
While turtles play cards, well into the night.
A sloth makes a pun, oh what a treat,
Racing to lunch while losing its feet!

So come and smile, as we uncover,
The waking world's laugh, it's like no other.
Each moment shines, full of glee,
In nature's antics, wild and free!

Celestial Cascade of Morning Splendor

A light show bursts, with laughter in bloom,
As beams of joy fill every room.
The clouds prank picnics, they drift on by,
Kite-surfing pelicans in the sky!

Palm fronds wave, in a playful cheer,
The penguins join, wearing their gear!
With sun hats on, and shades so bright,
They strut about, what a funny sight!

Each wave whispers tales of the shore,
While sunburnt crabs just beg for more.
The juice spills out, from a coconut spree,
As seagulls dance, 'Round a jolly tree!

So raise your glasses, let laughter ignite,
With friends all around, we bask in delight.
In this gentle glow, life's humor unfurls,
A cascade of fun, that twirls and whirls!

A Soothing Prelude of Light

Like a kitten yawning, the day stretches wide,
Bright hues of laughter, come along for the ride!
The sun rolls in, with a smile so sweet,
As waves crash down, tap dancing feet!

Palm leaves nod, with a winking glare,
Surprises await, even under a chair.
A pineapple wiggles, it's having a ball,
While turtles juggle, oh what a call!

Swaying grasses, with secrets to share,
Invite the day, with jovial flair.
The fireflies giggle, in warm evening's light,
As laughter echoes, into the night!

With dreams on the horizon, and fun in our sight,
We welcome this morn, so warm and bright.
So dance to the rhythm, feel free to ignite,
A soothing prelude, that feels just right!

Shimmering Waters Reflecting Light

The fish are splashing, doing flips,
While ducks are quacking silly quips.
A coconut falls, hits a lazy frog,
He croaks loud, in a morning jog.

A crab in shades and a beach hat,
Dancing the cha-cha, imagine that!
Sea turtles giggle as they glide,
In this bright world, there's no need to hide.

A lazy hammock swings with flair,
As seagulls laugh without a care.
Everything glimmers, takes the stage,
In this wacky dawn, we're all the rage!

Nature's Awakening in Pastel

The sky's a canvas, colors blend,
A parrot shrieks, making me bend.
The flowers yawn, stretching wide,
And all the bugs take a crazy ride.

A chubby monkey slips on a vine,
Sipping on juice, oh, how divine!
While toucans gossip in hues so bright,
Their jokes fall flat, but what a sight!

In this quirky realm of morning cheer,
Bright-eyed creatures draw near.
With giggles and grins, the day begins,
Whirling around like busy pins!

The Dance of Sunbeams

Light beams shimmy, like wigglin' worms,
As they tickle trees with playful squirms.
Butterflies twirl in a feathered show,
While coffee beans dance, brewing in tow.

A squirrel drops acorns, preparing for fun,
Saying, "Hey dude, let's frolic and run!"
The sun winks down, it's quite the tease,
Oh, what a sight, surely to please!

The world is laughing, so carefree,
Nature's party, for you and me.
With sparkly rays and giggly beams,
All our worries just drift like dreams!

Awakening Flora in the Amber Glow

Daisies yawn, stretch, say, "What's new?"
While petals gossip, as flowers just do.
A cactus blushes in the dawn's embrace,
As the breeze sways, they start a race.

The vines are tangled in a silly hug,
As bees play tag, giving hugs a tug.
Each bloom's a joker, with blooms so bright,
In this comedic garden, we feel the light.

So let's celebrate this comical show,
With every petal that starts to glow.
In this amber hue, let laughter unfurl,
As we dance with the flowers and join their whirl!

The Alchemy of Dawn and Dreams

As dawn spills yellow on sleepy streets,
The birds hold council, planning their tweets.
A squirrel juggles nuts with glee,
As if it's all part of a grand jamboree.

Pajamas dance in the morning breeze,
While coffee brews with a hint of tease.
The sun winks down, a cheeky lad,
At all the silliness, it's really not bad.

Shutters slam, a dog lets out a howl,
Awakening all with a mischievous growl.
The world spins bright, in playful jest,
What a way to wake, it's simply the best!

In the midst of giggles, the day comes alive,
As we stumble about, barely survive.
With joy in our hearts and socks not a pair,
We embrace the madness in morning's fair air.

Vibrations of Earth and Sky

The clouds are fluffy like cotton candy,
While roosters join in, their song quite dandy.
A jumping fish dreams of a grand ballet,
As the sun laughs, making shadows play.

The breeze tells jokes, it tickles your nose,
While flowers gossip in their colorful clothes.
A crab moonwalks, clumsy yet proud,
Dancing with joy, oh it's just so loud!

As nature chuckles, the trees sway and bend,
While I trip over roots that just won't mend.
Life's a circus under this vibrant dome,
Every creature finding its zany home.

In this chaos of colors, we laugh so bright,
Sipping on laughter while catching the light.
If skies could giggle, they surely would burst,
With all of this humor, we're never the worst!

Palette of the Rising Sun

The sun mixes colors like a playful chef,
A splash of orange, and a hint of clef.
Laughter ripples over ocean's face,
While jellyfish float with a curious grace.

Umbrellas unfold like flowers in bloom,
As beachgoers frolic, dispelling all gloom.
A crab in sunglasses surveys the scene,
Declaring himself the beach day's queen.

The sand tickles toes, a warm embrace,
As seagulls dive down to steal our space.
With flip-flops flapping, we race down the shore,
Chasing giggles, always wanting more.

In this riot of colors, we dance and we play,
Crafting memories that won't fade away.
For every sunrise is painted anew,
In this canvas of joy, my heart sings for you.

Caress of Daylight on Salted Air

Daylight stretches with a lazy yawn,
While waves whisper secrets, breaking at dawn.
A seagull steals breakfast, can you believe?
As I stand there, half lost, still trying to weave.

The salty breeze tussles my hair in a mess,
Making me feel like a haphazard princess.
As the sun winks at the goofy display,
I giggle in rhythm with the waves' ballet.

Children giggling, building castles of sand,
While snails fashion hats; it's all very grand.
A dolphin jumps in, putting on a show,
As I try to leap, but just stumble and go!

With sun-kissed cheeks and laughter abound,
The world spins funny; joy knows no bound.
So here's to the madness of day's bright affair,
Where sunlight and laughter dance in midair.

Golden Hues on Sandy Shores

Golden rays sneak through the trees,
Waking the crabs with a tickling breeze.
Seagulls squawk like they're on a spree,
Chasing the waves like they're chasing me.

Flip-flops fly off as I run to the bay,
A dolphin nods like it knows a good play.
Sandy pancakes for breakfast today,
With jellyfish dancing in their own ballet.

The sun yawns wide, it's a lazy sight,
Sipping its coffee, feeling just right.
A wavy dog barks at a kite in flight,
While sunbathers tease it with sheer delight.

Beach chairs fold up with a comical snap,
Sun hats wrestle, giving shade a slap.
Shells form a band, they all want to clap,
A party starts, let's all take a nap!

Morning's Kiss on Feathery Wings

Birds chirp loud, like they've lost their minds,
Flapping around with some silly finds.
A parrot mixes colors, it really grinds,
While others complain about morning's binds.

Fluffy clouds wear pajamas, what a sight,
As the sun tickles them with golden light.
An iguana struts, oh, isn't he bright?
A runway model, he'd win the fight!

The rooster crows, a punctual prank,
While the iguana's giving a rival a flank.
A toucan slurps nectar, he's quite the tank,
As butterflies flutter, they go to his bank.

All creatures join in a morning parade,
Spreading the laughter, decisions unmade.
With feathery friends, oh what a charade,
Every day's funny, let's not be delayed!

Radiance Over the Reefs

Corals are giggling, dressed in their best,
As sunlight plays, they take on a quest.
Fish in tuxedos swim with zest,
Trying to impress, they really invest.

A starfish winks like it owns the show,
While seaweed sways in a rhythmic flow.
Anemones wave, 'Come join our row!'
"Oh no!" says a crab, "Watch out for the blow!"

A clownfish jokes, 'I'm a real funny guy!'
While turtles race, giving it a try.
Jellyfish drift in a soft goodbye,
Tickling the fish passing by with a sigh.

The sun dives deep, as shadows expand,
A dolphin leaps high, isn't it grand?
With ripples of laughter that none can withstand,
The whole reef erupts, just like it had planned!

The Gentle Lullaby of Dawn

As sunlight creeps in, the world starts to grin,
Blankets of stars begin to thin.
A cat gives a stretch, 'Let the fun begin!'
While 'sleepy' is out, and 'let's play' moves in.

A sleepy head stirs with a yawn so wide,
Coffee cups dance, they're ready for pride.
The toaster pops up with a merry stride,
As bread lands crisp, happily fried.

Chickens in pajamas, what a sight to behold,
Doing a jig as the day starts to unfold.
The garden's all chuckles, its tales often told,
With sunshine and laughter, it's pure, unretrolled.

A gentle breeze blows, tickling the trees,
Nature's own laughter, a joyful tease.
As the day breaks through, with warmth it frees,
Let's all join in, the world's here to please!

Silhouettes of Heaven

Napping seagulls on the shore,
Coconut dreams they can't ignore.
Palm trees stretching in a dance,
Waving hello with a leafy glance.

Dolphins giggle, splash and play,
Messy hair on a bright display.
Sunscreen chaos on every face,
Under the sun's warm embrace.

Island Air

Whiffs of fruit twist through the breeze,
While pineapples pretend to tease.
The local catch jumps on the grill,
Flavors dancing, such a thrill!

A parrot squawks a morning tune,
Stealing jokes from the cartoon moon.
Beach towels tangled, what a sight,
As we laugh 'til the stars ignite.

Morning Sweet

Coffee spills over the rim,
As the roosters sing with a whim.
Sugar ants invade the feast,
Chasing crumbs like a tiny beast.

Pancakes flip with a happy flop,
As syrup waterfalls never stop.
We'll take a bite, then dance around,
Lost in giggles, joy profound.

A Canvas of Renewed Bliss

Brush strokes painted on the sky,
In colors that cause dreams to fly.
Every wave a playful cheer,
As the day whispers, 'Come near!'

Sunscreen suits with polka dots,
Strutting about with funky thoughts.
A rollercoaster of laughter grows,
With each splash, the fun just flows.

Soft Footprints on Warm Sand

Footprints left in a wobbly line,
Leading to where the sun will shine.
Sandcastles crumble with a roar,
While giggles echo on the shore.

Starfish laugh at our silly dance,
Seashells whisper, 'Take a chance!'
We chase the waves, a merry band,
With hope and joy, we make our stand.

The First Breath of Daybreak

Morning whispers with a grin,
The roosters crow, let the games begin.
Palm trees sway, looking fresh and bright,
As squirrels dance, what a silly sight.

Coconuts fall, with a thud, not a flinch,
The ocean giggles, is it time to pinch?
Flip-flops flapping on the sandy shore,
Come join the fun, who could ask for more?

Breeze tickles cheek, like a cheeky friend,
Laughter blooms as the day ascends.
Sunrise paints the sky with a wink,
Coffee brews; oh, we're on the brink!

With every beam, a smile unfurls,
As day rolls in to tickle our curls.
Bring out the fruit, let's toast with glee,
In this morning circus, just you and me.

Awakening Paradise in Palettes

Colors burst with a playful cheer,
Mandarins giggle; they're almost near.
Bananas wear sunglasses, oh what a sight,
As mangoes dance, feeling oh so bright.

Parrots squawk in shades of lime,
Sipping nectar, they take their time.
Cups of juice jump from side to side,
In this vivid world, come for the ride!

Fluffy clouds like marshmallows float,
The sun dons a hat, oh what a coat!
Laughter erupts from the leaves up high,
In this painter's dream, let's paint the sky!

Palette of joy, bursting at the seams,
Wake up, wake up, it's time for dreams.
In this quirky art, find your own way,
Let's splash in colors, it's our play day!

Gentle Murmurs at Dawn

Whispers of coffee tickle the air,
Butterflies twirl without a care.
Soft breezes gossip with the palms,
While crabs plot mischief—oh, the charms!

Waves chuckle as they tickle the shore,
Seashells giggle, begging for more.
A sleepy turtle nods, takes a stance,
In this morning jest, they all prance.

Sunrise winks, like a cheeky tease,
Birds dress up in polka-dot leaves.
With every rustle and tiny glow,
Nature laughs, putting on a show.

Crabs do the cha-cha; what a delight,
As sea stars shine in the warming light.
So bring on the giggles, let's have our say,
When soft whispers wrap up the day!

Warmth of the Newly Born Day

The sun peeks out, cheeky and bold,
While kittens stretch, searching for gold.
Warmth wraps around like a soft, fuzzy hug,
As the day stirs awake, what a snug rug!

Pancakes flip high, with syrupy flair,
As the toaster pops, sending crumbs in the air.
Colors invade from the east with a cheer,
Making us giggle, the morning is here!

Lemons roll underfoot, like happy marbles,
As chatter erupts over silly garbles.
Birds perform their morning ballet,
With feathers so bright, they steal the display!

On this glorious stage, let's shout hooray,
In the laughter of daybreak, come and play.
As warmth flows in, with rhythms to sway,
Let's dance through the joy of this brand new day!

www.ingramcontent.com/pod-product-compliance
Lightning Source LLC
Chambersburg PA
CBHW072117070526
44585CB00016B/1482